A GIFT FOR:

Crazy About Christmas

BARBOUR
PUBLISHING

CRAZY ABOUT CHRISTMAS™

COPYRIGHT © 2003 BY MARK GILROY COMMUNICATIONS, INC.
TULSA, OKLAHOMA

ART AND DESIGN BY JACKSONDESIGNCO,LLC
SILOAM SPRINGS, ARKANSAS

ISBN 1-59310-424-3

PUBLISHED BY BARBOUR PUBLISHING, INC., P.O. BOX 719,
UHRICHSVILLE, OHIO 44683, www.barbourpublishing.com

Member of the
Evangelical Christian
Publishers Association

PRINTED IN CHINA.

Crazy About Christmas

AND SHE BROUGHT FORTH
HER FIRSTBORN SON,
AND WRAPPED HIM
IN SWADDLING CLOTHS,
AND LAID HIM IN A MANGER.

LUKE 2:7

I'M CRAZY ABOUT CHRISTMAS
BECAUSE MY FAMILY ALWAYS
DECORATES THE TREE TOGETHER.

I'M CRAZY ABOUT CHRISTMAS
BECAUSE WE LOVE WAITING UP
FOR SANTA CLAUS.

I'M CRAZY ABOUT CHRISTMAS
BECAUSE OF "SECRET SANTA" PRESENTS.

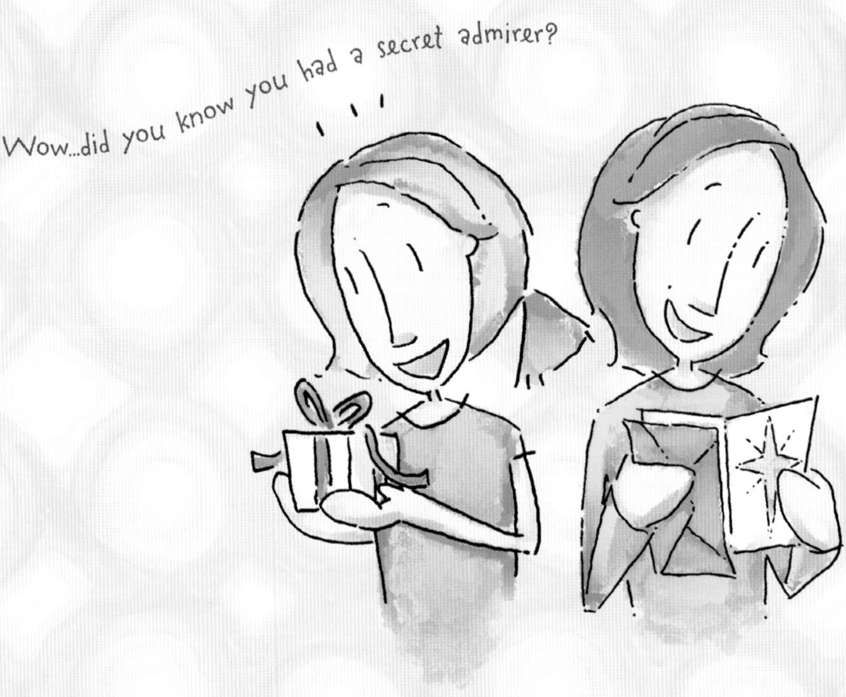
Wow...did you know you had a secret admirer?

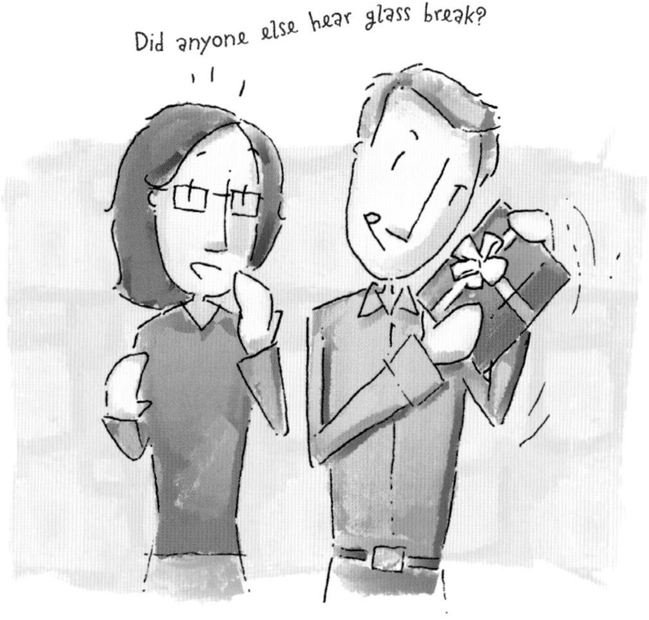
Did anyone else hear glass break?

I'M CRAZY ABOUT CHRISTMAS
BECAUSE IT'S SO MUCH FUN GUESSING
WHAT'S WRAPPED UP IN THE BOXES.

I'M CRAZY ABOUT CHRISTMAS
BECAUSE OF MISTLETOE.

I'M CRAZY ABOUT CHRISTMAS
BECAUSE OF ROARING FIRES.

(EVEN WHEN THEY AREN'T REAL.)

I'M CRAZY ABOUT CHRISTMAS
BECAUSE OF HOT CHOCOLATE
AND MARSHMALLOWS.

I'M CRAZY ABOUT CHRISTMAS BECAUSE
IT IS PURE JOY TO DO NICE THINGS
FOR MY CHILDREN.

I'M CRAZY ABOUT CHRISTMAS
BECAUSE OF FRESH-CUT PINE TREES.

I'M CRAZY ABOUT CHRISTMAS
BECAUSE OF ROAD TRIPS
TO SEE FAMILY.

I'M CRAZY ABOUT CHRISTMAS
BECAUSE OUR FAMILY WORKS
ON PROJECTS TOGETHER.

The family that licks together...sticks together.

I'M CRAZY ABOUT CHRISTMAS
BECAUSE OF THE UNFORGETTABLE
CHILDREN'S PAGEANTS AT CHURCH.

I'M CRAZY ABOUT CHRISTMAS
BECAUSE OF MY DAD'S COOL
HOLIDAY TIES.

I'M CRAZY ABOUT CHRISTMAS
BECAUSE OF THE BEAUTIFUL
SOUNDS OF THE SEASON.

I'M CRAZY ABOUT CHRISTMAS
BECAUSE IT'S A TIME TO GROW
AS AN INDIVIDUAL.

I'M CRAZY ABOUT CHRISTMAS
BECAUSE OF THE DECORATIONS
AND LIGHTS.

I'M CRAZY ABOUT CHRISTMAS
BECAUSE OF THE FUN PARTIES
WE GET INVITED TO.

I'm dreaming of a whi-i-i-i-te Christmas.

I'M CRAZY ABOUT CHRISTMAS
BECAUSE OF ALL THE GREAT
TV SPECIALS.

I'M CRAZY ABOUT CHRISTMAS
BECAUSE OF AUNT GERALDINE'S
WORLD FAMOUS FRUITCAKE.

I'M CRAZY ABOUT CHRISTMAS
BECAUSE THE WHOLE COMMUNITY
COMES TOGETHER.

I'M CRAZY ABOUT CHRISTMAS
BECAUSE OUR NEIGHBORHOOD REALLY
GETS INTO THE HOLIDAY SPIRIT.

I'M CRAZY ABOUT CHRISTMAS
BECAUSE IT'S FUN TO SEE HOW
EXCITED THE KIDS GET.

I'M CRAZY ABOUT CHRISTMAS
BECAUSE I LOVE DECORATING COOKIES.

Okay, so on to page three...
"Johnny, now six, is the very
best speller in his class, and..."

I'M CRAZY ABOUT CHRISTMAS
BECAUSE IT'S GREAT TO CATCH UP ON
WHAT'S HAPPENING WITH OLD FRIENDS.

I'M CRAZY ABOUT CHRISTMAS
BECAUSE OF THE WONDERFUL MUSIC.

It's beginning to look a lot like Christmas...

We have a third and seven from the twelve.

I'M CRAZY ABOUT CHRISTMAS
BECAUSE IT IS A SPECIAL TIME FOR
FAMILY MEMBERS TO BE TOGETHER.

I'M CRAZY ABOUT CHRISTMAS
BECAUSE OF MEETING FAMILY
MEMBERS I NEVER KNEW I HAD.

I'M CRAZY ABOUT CHRISTMAS
BECAUSE EVERYONE EXPRESSES
GOODWILL TO ONE ANOTHER.

I'M CRAZY ABOUT CHRISTMAS
BECAUSE IT IS WONDERFUL BOTH
TO GIVE AND TO RECEIVE.

I'M CRAZY ABOUT CHRISTMAS
BECAUSE KIDS ARE ANGELIC
THIS TIME OF YEAR.

I'M CRAZY ABOUT CHRISTMAS
BECAUSE MEN GET TO ACT
LIKE LITTLE BOYS.

I'M CRAZY ABOUT CHRISTMAS
BECAUSE OF WONDERFUL GIFTS
FROM GRANDMAS.

I'M CRAZY ABOUT CHRISTMAS
BECAUSE OF FAMILY PICTURES.

And yes, we are going to keep taking pictures until everyone smiles!

I'M CRAZY ABOUT CHRISTMAS
BECAUSE THERE'S ALWAYS
PLENTY OF FOOD TO EAT.

I'M CRAZY ABOUT CHRISTMAS
BECAUSE IT IS A WONDERFUL TIME TO
HELP THOSE WHO HAVE SPECIAL NEEDS.

I'M CRAZY ABOUT CHRISTMAS
BECAUSE OF CANDLELIGHT
SERVICES AT CHURCH.

I'M CRAZY ABOUT CHRISTMAS
BECAUSE BABIES SEEM EVEN MORE
SPECIAL THAN AT OTHER
TIMES OF THE YEAR.

I'M CRAZY ABOUT CHRISTMAS
BECAUSE THE STARS SEEM
A LITTLE BIT BRIGHTER.

I'M CRAZY ABOUT CHRISTMAS
BECAUSE WE ALL ARE INVITED TO
RECEIVE THE GREATEST GIFT OF ALL.

I'M CRAZY ABOUT CHRISTMAS
BECAUSE THE OLD STORIES
SEEM BRAND-NEW EVERY YEAR.

I'M CRAZY ABOUT CHRISTMAS
BECAUSE IT PROMISES HOPE
EVEN AFTER A TOUGH YEAR.

I'M CRAZY ABOUT CHRISTMAS
BECAUSE OF WONDERFUL MEMORIES
OF THE YEAR—AND OF A LIFETIME!

I'M CRAZY ABOUT CHRISTMAS
BECAUSE EVEN SOLDIERS STOP
FIGHTING FOR ONE DAY OF THE YEAR.

I'M CRAZY ABOUT CHRISTMAS
BECAUSE EVEN PEOPLE
WHO DON'T SING VERY WELL
SOUND WONDERFUL!

I'M CRAZY ABOUT CHRISTMAS
BECAUSE OF JESUS.

I bring you good tidings of great joy which will be to all people.

FOR THERE
IS BORN
TO YOU
THIS DAY
IN THE CITY
OF DAVID
A SAVIOR,
WHO IS
CHRIST
THE LORD.

LUKE 2:10–11

ALSO AVAILABLE:

CRAZY ABOUT MISTLETOE

CRAZY ABOUT MY CAT

CRAZY ABOUT MY DAUGHTER

CRAZY ABOUT MY DOG

CRAZY ABOUT MY FRIEND

CRAZY ABOUT MY GRANDPARENTS

CRAZY ABOUT MY SISTER

CRAZY ABOUT MY MOM

CRAZY ABOUT MY DAD

CRAZY ABOUT MY HUSBAND

CRAZY ABOUT MY WIFE

CRAZY ABOUT YOU

CRAZY ABOUT MY TEACHER

CRAZY ABOUT CHOCOLATE